JEREZ DE LA FRONTERA, OCTOBER 26, 1997 - 2.00 PM

JEREZ DE LA FRONTERA, OCTOBER 26, 1997 - 3.45 PM

PHOTOGRAPHS BY
GIANNI GIANSANTI

jacques villeneuve

Project and artistic direction by Roberto Bettoni

ques
neuve

A CHAMPION IN PICTURES

Text by Cédric Daetwyler

Layout Alessandra Aletti   **Translation** Branson Atterbury & Barrie McWhirter

Jacques Villeneuve. Legend? Hero? Star? Maybe. But, a far cry from the stereotype of a pre-programmed champion? Undoubtedly. He is essentially a normal human being, a person who is in touch with the times but different in one way: he belongs to the rare breed that is the Formula 1 racing driver.

He loves to take risks and pushes himself to the limit, even to the point of danger. Born into motor racing, he has grown up with roaring engines and has imbibed pure speed. But out of his fireproof overalls and away from the atmosphere of the paddock, he retains his normal identity. He fiercely defends his right to privacy and runs his life as discreetly as possible. Only a few close friends get a glimpse of the young champion's private moments.

What you see is what you get with the young Villeneuve. He likes a laugh, he likes to have fun and indulge himself in his great passions: skiing in the Swiss Alps, music, computers and reading. He lives life to the full, fast as the racing cars he drives, Jacques Villeneuve makes the most of every minute of free time. Though this is becoming rarer due to mounting work schedules.

Adored by his fans but also criticised, Jacques Villeneuve can inspire passion whilst upsetting the most conservative and purist of F1 followers. With his hair bleached platinum blonde, he has become the enfant terrible of the track, someone with his own views who is not slow to challenge a decision he considers wrong.

It was 1996 when he began in Formula 1. He arrived from the States and IndyCars

where he won everything in his second season - the Indianapolis 500 and a World Championship. As the youngest-ever driver to dominate the series he had nothing left to prove. And so the road led him to Formula 1 where his father, Gilles, had left the legacy of the Villeneuve name. Establishing himself in his own right soon became a priority and, as strategic planning is second nature, Jacques Villeneuve knew the answer was to start winning as soon as he could.

From his very first Grand Prix in Australia in March 1996, where he amazingly took pole and finished second having led for most of the race, Jacques knew what he had to do. Winning the season's fourth Grand Prix at the Nürburgring in Germany, he proved that he was a serious contender. Since then he has established himself, grown in confidence and pushed his limits further. If you are a Villeneuve and you take the decision to drive in F1, there can be no excuse for mistakes or failure. Through his wit and daring, he has avoided all the pitfalls.

Smiled on by fortune, Jacques Villeneuve has, suddenly and reluctantly, became a star. He is today considered a modern hero.

The real Jacques is revealed in these pages: his private moments, the happy times and those of great disappointment; the man before the camera shares those emotions and memories.

This story is about a Champion, unique in his own right, a truly legendary figure.

Discovery

■ **DRESSING IN THE MOTORHOME BEFORE STARTING WINTER TESTING.**

Jacques Villeneuve enters Formula 1 with Williams. Before him, great drivers like Nigel Mansell, Alain Prost and Ayrton Senna have been the powerhouse of the prestigious English team. At 24 the youngest ever IndyCar World Champion has to familiarise himself with his new environment.

"I did over 8.000 kilometres in my Williams Renault before the 1996 season began. As it was lighter and more responsive than my single-seater in Indy, I had to get used to the new feel. The more kilometres I put in, the more I knew how to handle the new sensations. Once in total harmony with my car, I was ready to push it to its limit."

■ A MOMENT TO STUDY THE

TELEMETRY DURING TESTING.

"The new season gets under way during the winter. It's sometimes
Testing in all conditions will bring wins in the future and that's my

difficult to get motivated when it's cold and wet.
motivation on a grey day."

■ ANOTHER HARD DAY'S

WORK OVER.

"Breakfast is a ritual: ice cold milk, cereal, two fried eggs, French toast with maple syrup and a roll with peanut butter and chocolate spread. No matter where I am I eat the same thing. It's the last moment of calm before we start up our engines."

Learning

From his first Grand Prix in Australia, Jacques proved an opponent to be reckoned with by his rivals. As a rookie he learnt circuits over a race weekend often having to adapt to changing conditions, which would dramatically affect race strategy at the last minute. Talent does not always make up for inexperience, but making mistakes helps him to perfect his driving skills.

■ THE START OF THE BRAZILIAN GRAND PRIX IMMEDIATELY AFTER A HUGE DOWNPOUR.

Rothmans
Williams RENAULT
elf
Rothmans
GOODYEAR
Rothmans RACING
Rothmans
RENAULT
elf
Rothmans
SONAX
MIRAGE
GRANITO CERAMICO

■ THE EMERGING JACQUES VILLENEUVE AND THE EXPERIENCED DAMON HILL, BOTH SONS OF RACING HEROES AND FULL OF RESPECT FOR EACH OTHER ... BUT JACQUES WAS THE MORE IMPRESSIVE IN AUSTRALIA, THE FIRST GRAND PRIX OF THE SEASON, WHERE HE PROVED HIMSELF TO BE MORE THAN AN ASPIRING NUMBER TWO.

■ IN THE CHANGING ROOMS AT INTERLAGOS AFTER QUALIFYING THIRD.

 BACK TO THE
HOTEL ... THE
CHAOS OF SÃO
PAULO BELOW.

▶▶ TIME TO RELAX
AFTER LUNCH IN
THE HOTEL ROOM
IN BUENOS AIRES.

"Being on my own for a moment helps me to focus, gather my wits and look at my mistakes before having to talk to the journalists and answer all their questions."

A live wire

"To have time to myself is a luxury." Far too rare these days, and therefore precious, Jacques Villeneuve fights to keep these moments private and to do what he enjoys most. Away from the Formula 1 scene, at home in Monaco or skiing in Switzerland his life is non-stop. Every day is packed and sport plays an important part, a racing driver constantly has to stay in shape. Music, reading, role-playing games, computers and evenings with friends take up the rest of his time. Fiercely independent, extremely passionate and always on the move, he powers through the day with an abundant vitality.

"I love playing arcade games.
It's a good test of **reflexes**, but also
helps me prepare for Grands Prix."

"I'll tell you a story. I have been accused of being a **danger to the public** on my roller-blades and was fined by the police."

"I don't like pumping iron in a gym, I'd rather **run in the fresh air,** it clears my head at the same time."

"Getting together with **my family** has become something I manage far too rarely."

"I read a lot. My tastes vary from magazines to literature. If possible, I avoid F1 reviews."

" It's important not to have **an accident** when going for it "

"Once I set myself a challenge I must prove I have the **resources** necessary to overcome it."

" **W**inter means skiing,
snow and Villars in Switzerland,
where I spent part of my childhood."

"With skiing you have to adjust to your surroundings - a bit like F1."

"**S**andrine is sanity in a mad world." *Le Figaro Magazine 8/3/1997*

■ Monaco

Out for a Win

Out of three Grands Prix, Jacques notched up two second places (in Australia and Argentina) and arrived in Europe more determined than ever. At the Nürburgring in Germany he kept Michael Schumacher at bay and his fourth Grand Prix saw his first Formula 1 victory. The ensuing races meant that there was no time to relax. San Marino and Monaco were to give the young talent a taste of disappointment with two consecutive retirements. He would have to wait until Spain and Canada to get on the podium again, finishing third and second respectively.

■ A SPLENDID VIEW OF THE MONTE CARLO CIRCUIT.

▶ THE CROWDS GATHER IN MONTREAL TO SEE THEIR YOUNG COMPATRIOT.

■ His father, Gilles Villeneuve, won his first Grand Prix in Montreal in 1978.

◄ Refuelling and a tyre
change during the
Canadian Grand Prix.

"To race in Montreal is special,
though my feelings are always mixed.
I'm happy to be back in Quebec but
there is intense pressure from the media.
My first Grand Prix on home-ground - and
it was a relief to get into the car."

■ THE BELGIAN CIRCUIT OF SPA-FRANCORCHAMPS, IN THE HEART OF THE FOREST.

■ A GOOD LUCK MESSAGE FROM A FAN AT THE END OF THE CANADIAN GRAND PRIX.

■ SCENES OF ENTHUSIASM
AS THE CROWD GREETS
JACQUES VILLENEUVE'S
ARRIVAL IN MONZA.

"I'm fascinated by the passion of my fans. I'm in awe of their enthusiasm."

The master

To drive a Williams is synonymous with status. A new driver signed by Frank Williams must prove he can win races in one of the most competitive cars in Formula 1. Nothing satisfies Frank Williams but winning.

In the two years that Jacques has been with the team, he has won eleven Grands Prix and one World Championship. Frank describes Jacques as having talent, intelligence and a cool head. This relationship between the most outspoken and the most reserved men in the paddock is clearly a winning Formula.

▶ AN EXCHANGE OF OPINIONS BETWEEN JACQUES AND FRANK AT THE END OF A DAY'S TESTING IN IMOLA.

▶▶ FINAL PREPARATIONS BEFORE THE START OF THE ARGENTINE GRAND PRIX.

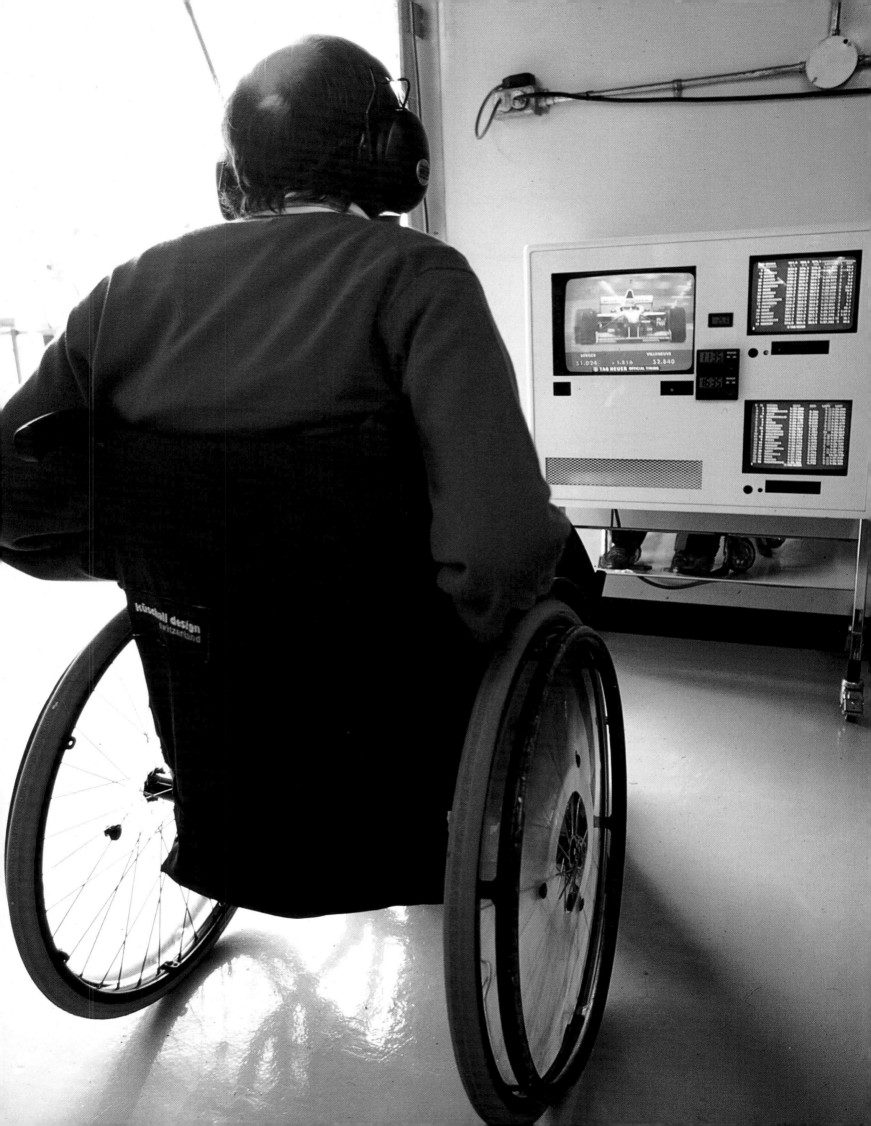

Rothmans
Rothmans
RACING
Rothmans
RACING
Rothmans
RACING
Rothmans
ANYO
YEAR

" I have an excellent relationship with Frank Williams. I can relax and say what I think to him. I am convinced that being open and honest at work is vital if we are to get good results."

■SUZUKA - JAPAN

The decider

Jacques now had four wins to his name and several top six finishes which put him nine points behind Damon Hill. For Jacques to win the Drivers' World Championship in Japan, Damon had to finish outside the top six and he himself had to take first. Unfortunately, a wheel from his car flew off and with it his only hope of clinching the world title. The race ended in disappointment, but a string of good results through the season confirmed the young outsider's talent.

■ THE BUILD-UP TO THE JAPANESE GRAND PRIX AT SUZUKA.

■ DAVID COULTHARD LATE

FOR THE GROUP PHOTO.

<u>LEFT</u>: JACQUES

SHARES A JOKE WITH

DAMON AND JOCK.

■ His race over,
Jacques can only
watch as team-mate
Damon Hill is
crowned World
Champion.
Right: Tears of joy
from Damon Hill's
wife, Georgie.

"I had to accept that this was Damon's day. He had a perfect race and deserved the title. I was happy for him because, although rivals, we were in the same team and had become friends during the season."

"I managed to persuade Mika and David that shaven heads would make them more aerodynamic."

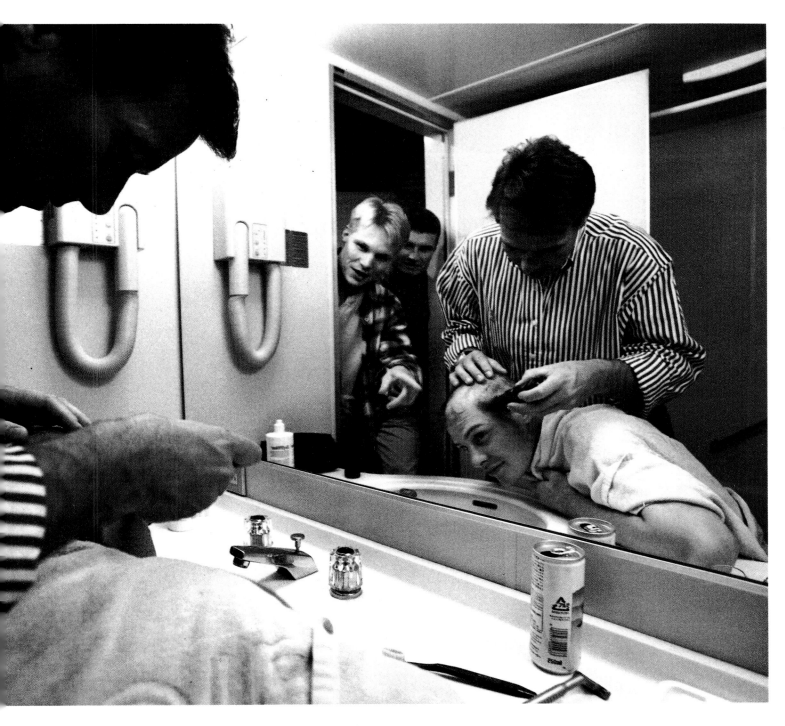

■ A NEW LOOK FOR
JACQUES, DAVID AND
MIKA TO CELEBRATE THE
END OF THE
CHAMPIONSHIP.

SOMEWHERE IN THE SKIES OVER EUROPE,

The mentor

In 1992 Jacques asked Craig, who had originally been a teacher at his school in Switzerland to be his manager. Like Jacques, Craig is a man of his word and equals him in determination. This synergy has enabled Jacques to make the most of his talent. The result is a strong team built on friendship and mutual respect.

CRAIG POLLOCK IS
ONE OF JACQUES'
CLOSEST FRIENDS AS
WELL AS BEING HIS
PERSONAL MANAGER.

"Alot of people are intrigued by our relationship. Craig is, above all, my best friend but he understands my difficult personality and knows how to get the best out of me."

The World Championship

Jacques had a clearly stated objective in his second Formula 1 season - to win the World Championship. This was distinctly possible: he had finished runner-up in his first year, the car was performing well, winter testing was promising and all the experience of 1996 was in his favour. He was the front runner and it only remained to identify the strongest challenger. Everybody was hoping for a title showdown with Michael Schumacher and the two soon found themselves pitted against each other for the Championship title.

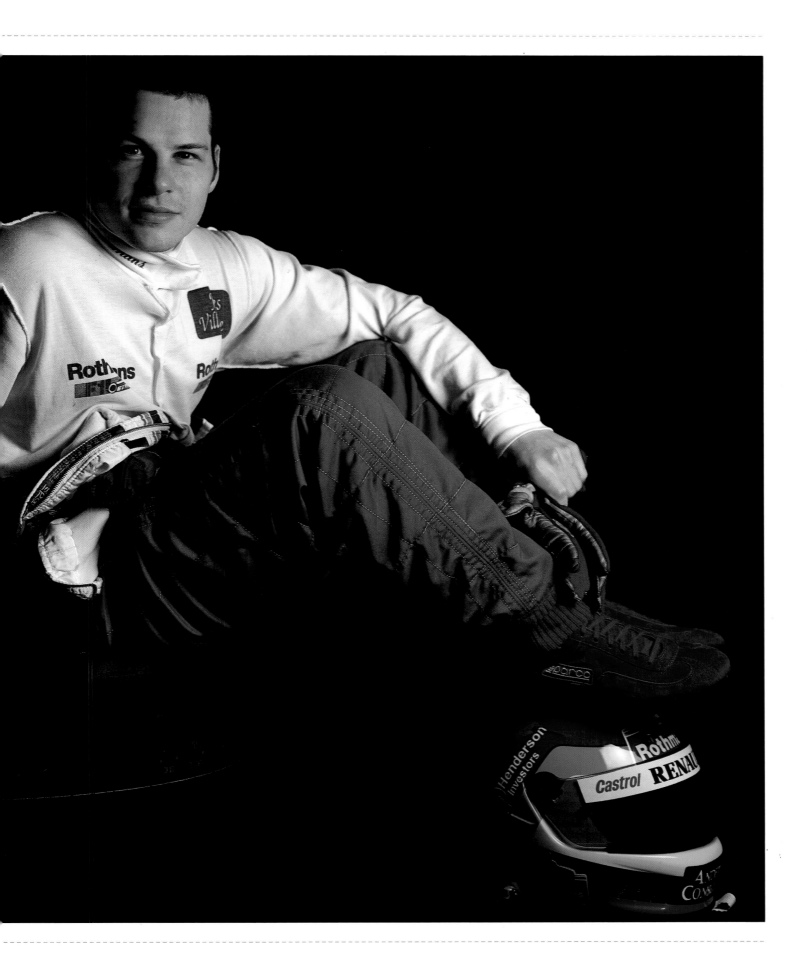

◀◀ A PAUSE DURING
THE 1997 OFFICIAL
PHOTO SHOOT.

◀ LAST MINUTE
PREPARATIONS
BEFORE CLIMBING
INTO THE CAR.

■ TESTING THE STEERING
WHEEL AND THE SEAT
IN THE NEW FW19
AT LE CASTELLET.

" The new car was late but proved itself quick and very competitive. For the first Grand Prix, I was on pole and ready for battle."

Obstacles to success

In Australia, Jacques was taken off at the first corner by Eddie Irvine but was quickly back on target with strong performances in Brazil and Argentina. By the first European race at Imola everything was looking good, he was confident, leading the Championship and had overcome the pressure at the beginning of the season. Then an electrical fault in the gearbox forced an early retirement and for the second year running he failed to finish. Two weeks later misfortune would strike again in Monaco, where he fell foul of the team's inaccurate weather forecast and did not last the race.

■ On the straight leading to Piratella just after the start of the San Marino Grand Prix.

" **W**hen we are stopped, I remain calm but every second seems like an eternity. All I can do is sit tight and hope the guys work as fast as they can."

■ WILLIAMS, FERRARI

AND JORDAN MECHANICS

IN A RACE AGAINST

THE CLOCK.

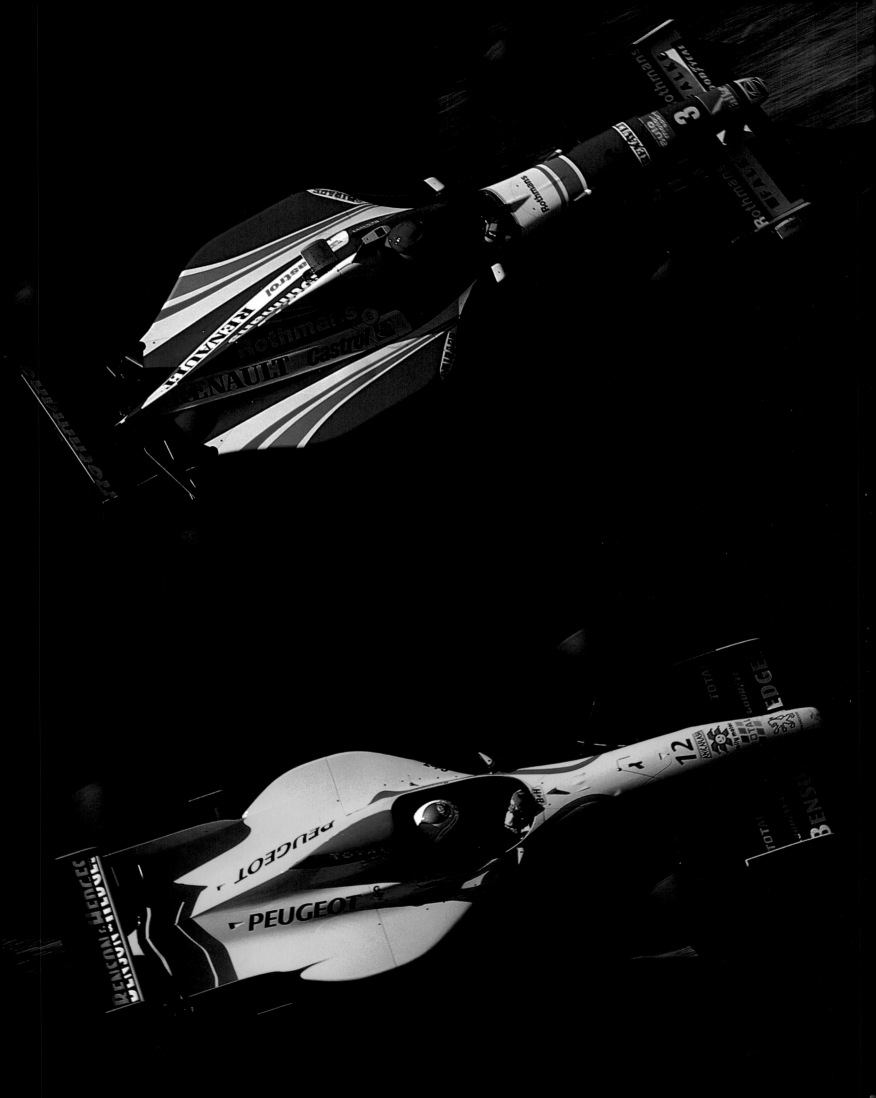

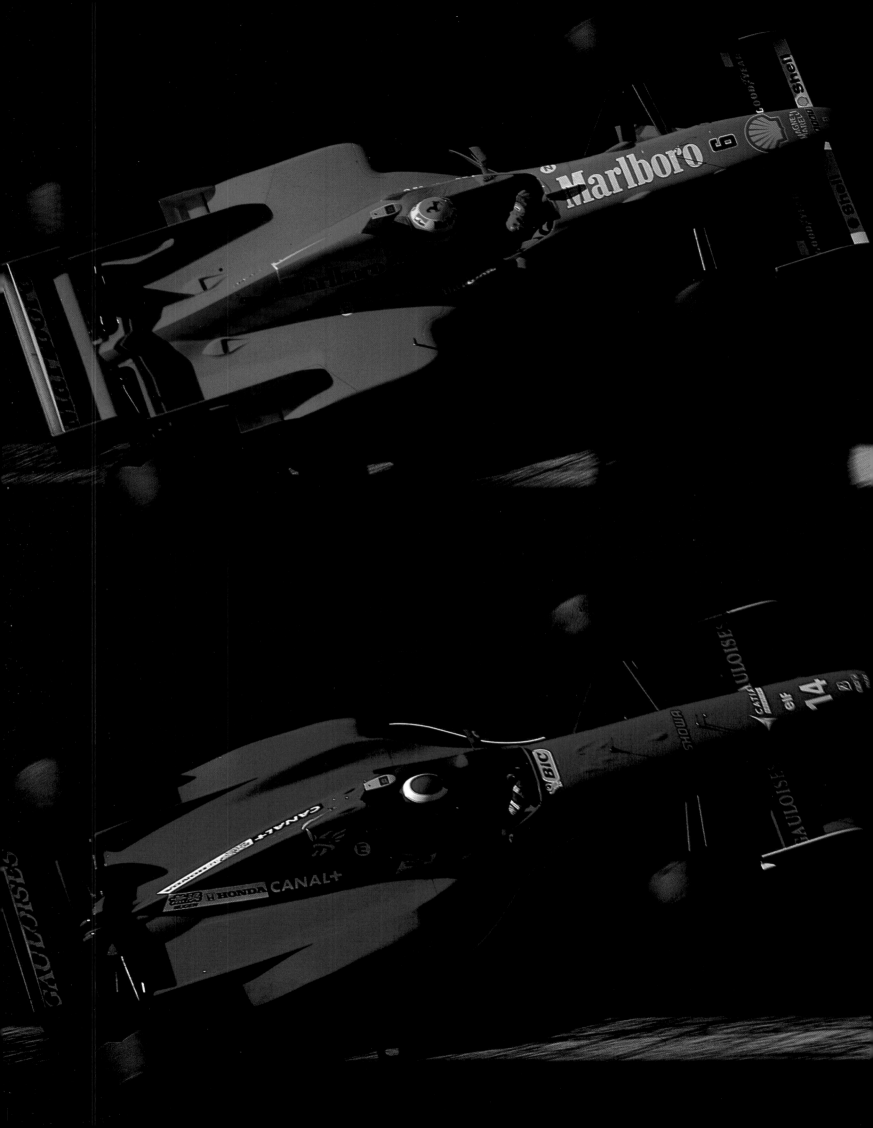

■ PASSING THE LOEWS CURVE, IMMEDIATELY AFTER THE MUNICIPAL CASINO.

"When the rain began it was obvious it was settling in and a dry set up on a wet track is like ice skating without the skates. Bad strategy had cost us dear. Disaster."

JACQUES VILLENEUVE
CELEBRATING HIS
THIRD VICTORY OF THE
SEASON ON THE PODIUM
IN BARCELONA.

THE MECHANICS WATCH THE SCREENS IN SPA.

Behind the scenes

T his is teamwork. Behind Jacques, there is the technical support and backup of an entire team working on the various set ups, who are prepared to put in long, hard hours to improve the car's performance. If Jacques often talks of "we" it is because every decision is made in conjunction with the team and everyone shares in the victory.

▶ A COMPLETE UNDERSTANDING WITH HIS RACE ENGINEER, JOCK CLEAR, IS THE KEY TO SUCCESS.

■ Testing - Le Castellet, France.

<u>Left</u> : Jock Clear oversees the proceedings.

▶ A massage

from his trainer,

Erwin Göllner.

" You forge team spirit

not with your team mate, but

with the engineers and

mechanics who work on the car."

A lacklustre Summer

Following his success in the Spanish Grand Prix, Jacques was upbeat about going to Canada and winning on his home turf. But his comments on the new rules brought fresh controversy and two days before practice began he was called before the FIA in Paris. Tired as a result of the pressures of the weekend, he failed to deliver in Quebec and back in Europe could only manage fourth at Magny-Cours. These poor performances helped Michael Schumacher take the lead in the Championship.

■ THE START OF THE FRENCH GRAND PRIX, MAGNY-COURS.

■ Tyre and brake performance are crucial.

" The tyre war is good for Formula 1 because the manufacturers constantly have to upgrade their compounds."

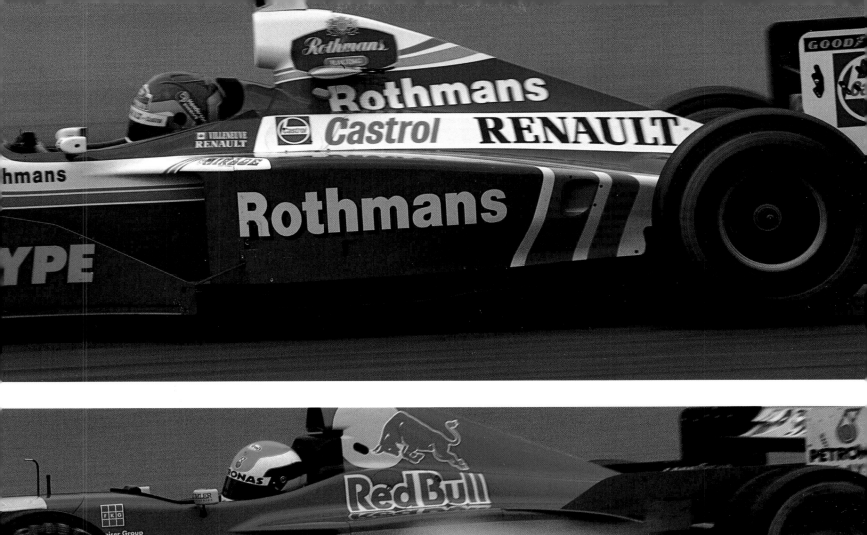

" **W**hat a weekend! Racing against Damon brought back great memories until his engine problem allowed me to pass him one lap from the end. He deserved to win but I really needed those ten points for the Championship. "

◄◄◄ THE BLEACHED LOOK CAUSES A STIR IN MAGNY-COURS.

◄◄ MICHAEL SCHUMACHER CLIMBS OUT OF HIS FERRARI DURING QUALIFYING FOR THE GERMAN GRAND PRIX.

◄ VILLENEUVE FLASHES PAST THE STANDS IN HOCKENHEIM IN THE WILLIAMS.

■ A MECHANICAL FAILURE ON

DAMON'S CAR ENABLED

JACQUES TO OVERTAKE HIM ON

THE LAST LAP AND WIN THE

HUNGARIAN GRAND PRIX.

LEFT: THE HUNGARORING

AT ITS HIGHEST POINT.

■ LEAVING THE GARAGE TO
LINE UP FOR THE ITALIAN
GRAND PRIX.

BELOW: THE REGULATION
SOFTWARE FOR THE CAR.

RIGHT: AFTER MONZA,
JACQUES AND JOCK WERE
DISAPPOINTED NOT HAVE
SCORED MORE POINTS.

▶ CHAMPANGE CELEBRATIONS
IN AUSTRIA AS JACQUES
LEADS MICHAEL
SCHUMACHER IN THE
CHAMPIONSHIP AGAIN.

"In spite of all the hard
work we put in, I performed poorly.
Even though the gap between
Michael and myself
was reduced, I
could not be
satisfied
coming fifth."

SANDRINE

A modern couple

Unlike the stereotypical Formula 1 girlfriend, Sandrine has her own life and does not live in her boyfriend's shadow. Jacques always says: "I couldn't respect a girlfriend who had no ambition." Frequently apart, their time together is all the more precious.

■ More telemetry, this time with Sandrine.

■ In between practice sessions for the race in Buenos Aires.

◀ Together in the hotel

after the Canadian

Grand Prix.

▶ A light lunch

together before

starting the Argentine

Grand Prix.

"It's really important to have someone so close. I know she's here for no other reason than to be with me."

Nadir

Failure to heed a waved yellow flag and a race ban in Japan left a bitter taste. He was allowed to race under threat of disqualification due to an appeal, which was dropped a few days later. Michael Schumacher again led the Championship and Jacques, one point behind, could not afford to leave anything to chance. These are the events, which preceded the final showdown at Jerez in Spain.

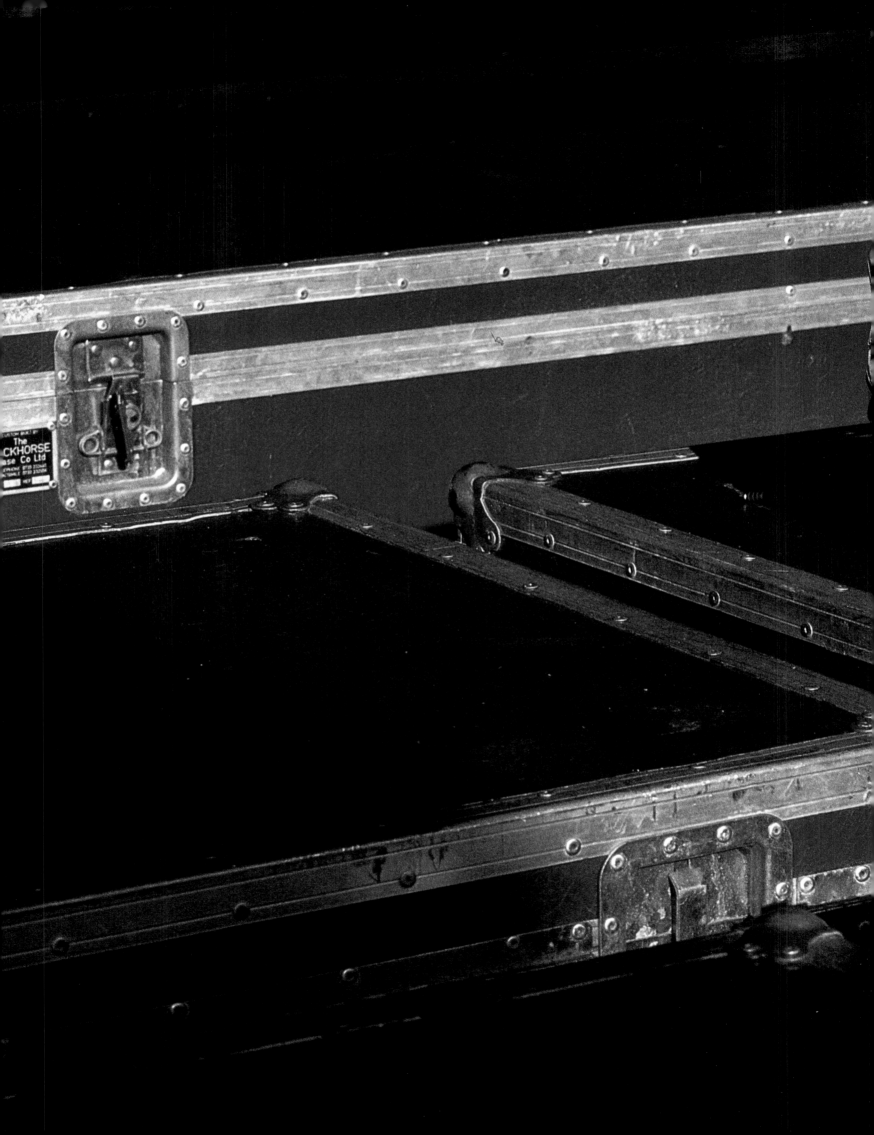

JEREZ DE LA FRONTERA

Epilogue

A mid the turmoil of the most important weekend of his life when he had everything at stake, Jacques' self-confidence helped him remain focused on the job in hand. In spite of the nightmare in Japan and mounting pressures he had overcome, Jacques was feeling stoic and serene. Intense media harrassment over the Villeneuve/Schumacher battle failed to rattle him and he kept his composure throughout practice. He knew that his team had pulled out all the stops to provide him with the best car they could. The team effort had been supreme, never before so positive; losing simply was not an option.

Jacques never gave up, even when the odds were stacked against him.

It was a hard fight but he came through.

The title was his once and for all.

■ A QUICK CALL TO JOANN, HIS MOTHER. CONGRATULATIONS FROM DAMON HILL AND THEN THE OFFICIAL PHOTOGRAPH OF THE NEW WORLD CHAMPION.

Jac
Ville

For
W
Cha

GIANCARLO FISICHELLA

JEAN ALESI

GIANNI MORBIDELLI

JARNO TRULLI

HEINZ- HARALD FRENTZEN

JACQUES VILLENEUVE

MIKA SALO

MICHAEL SCHUMACHER

RALF SCHUMACHER

MIKA HAKKINEN

UKYO KATAYAMA

OLIVIER PANIS

JOS VERSTAPPEN

SHINJI NAKANO

EDDIE IRVINE

DAMON HILL

TARSO MARQUES

DAVID COULTHARD

JAN MAGNUSSEN

JOHNNY HERBERT

GERHARD BERGER

"Y ou put yourself

before

everything else

he pressure of photographers and reporters, even if it distracts my

concentration, shows that I am doing an excellent job». São Paulo, Brazil, March 1

First published in
1997 by Goldstar
Holdings
Corporation

Copyright 1997
Goldstar Holdings
Corporation

© Photographs
Gianni Giansanti

Produced under
licence from Goldstar
Holdings Corporation

Printed in Italy by Grafedit
Spa
Azzano San Paolo, Bergamo.
Colour separation
by Fotolito Star
Bergamo

Prints Black & White
by Claudio Bassi - Rome.

Acknowledgements:
Goldstar Holdings
Corporation would like
to thank:
Belinda Olins, Fiona
McWhirter, Barbara
Pollock and Tim Sice at
Stellar Management.
Anne-Lise Daetwyler
and Bettina Clivaz.
ISBN : 976-8108-12-6